INFORMATIONS

NAME

ADDRESS

E-MAIL ADDRESS

WEBSITE

PHONE   FAX

EMERGENCY CONTACT PERSON

PHONE   FAX

LOG BOOK DETAILS

CONTINUED FROM LOG BOOK

LOG START DATE

CONTINUED TO LOG BOOK

LOG END DATE

Dedication

This Sailing Log Book is dedicated to all the sailors out there who love sailing and want to document their findings in the process.

You are my inspiration for producing books and I'm honored to be a part of keeping all of your sailing notes and records organized.

This journal notebook will help you record the details about your sailboat adventures.

Thoughtfully put together with these sections to record: Destination, Weather, Sea Conditions, Course, Speed, Distance, Navigation Notes, Days Run, Fuel on Board, Crew, Guest, Captain, & much more!

How to Use this Book

The purpose of this book is to keep all of your Sailing notes all in one place. It will help keep you organized.

This Sailing Log Book will allow you to accurately document every detail about your sailing adventures.

Here are examples of the prompts for you to fill in and write about your experience in this book:

1. Date & Destination

2. Weather, Forecast, Wind, Visibility, Sea Conditions

3. Time & ETA

4. Course

5. Speed

6. Distance

7. Navigation Notes

8. Events & Observations

9. Time Completed

10. Days Run

11. Average Speed

12. Fuel on Board

13. Crew & Guests

14. Captain

Sailing Log Book

DATE _____   DESTINATION _____

WEATHER _____   FORECAST _____

WIND _____   VISIBILITY _____

SEA CONDITIONS _____   ETA _____

TIME	COURSE	SPEED	DISTANCE	NAVIGATION NOTES	REMARKS

EVENTS / OBSERVATIONS

....
....
....
....
....
....
....

TIME COMPLETED _____   DAYS RUN _____

AVERAGE SPEED _____   FUEL ON BOARD _____

CREW & GUESTS

....
....
....
....

CAPTAIN _____

Sailing Log Book

DATE

DESTINATION

WEATHER

FORECAST

WIND

VISIBILITY

SEA CONDITIONS

ETA

TIME	COURSE	SPEED	DISTANCE	NAVIGATION NOTES	REMARKS

EVENTS / OBSERVATIONS

TIME COMPLETED

DAYS RUN

AVERAGE SPEED

FUEL ON BOARD

CREW & GUESTS

CAPTAIN

Sailing Log Book

DATE _____   DESTINATION _____

WEATHER _____   FORECAST _____

WIND _____   VISIBILITY _____

SEA CONDITIONS _____   ETA _____

TIME	COURSE	SPEED	DISTANCE	NAVIGATION NOTES	REMARKS

EVENTS / OBSERVATIONS

....
....
....
....
....
....
....

TIME COMPLETED _____   DAYS RUN _____

AVERAGE SPEED _____   FUEL ON BOARD _____

CREW & GUESTS

....
....
....
....

CAPTAIN _____

Sailing Log Book ☸

DATE .... DESTINATION ....

WEATHER .... FORECAST ....

WIND .... VISIBILITY ....

SEA CONDITIONS .... ETA ....

TIME	COURSE	SPEED	DISTANCE	NAVIGATION NOTES	REMARKS

EVENTS / OBSERVATIONS

....
....
....
....
....
....
....

TIME COMPLETED .... DAYS RUN ....

AVERAGE SPEED .... FUEL ON BOARD ....

CREW & GUESTS

....
....
....
....

CAPTAIN

Sailing Log Book

DATE _____ DESTINATION _____

WEATHER _____ FORECAST _____

WIND _____ VISIBILITY _____

SEA CONDITIONS _____ ETA _____

TIME	COURSE	SPEED	DISTANCE	NAVIGATION NOTES	REMARKS

EVENTS / OBSERVATIONS

....
....
....
....
....
....
....

TIME COMPLETED _____ DAYS RUN _____

AVERAGE SPEED _____ FUEL ON BOARD _____

CREW & GUESTS

....
....
....
....

CAPTAIN _____

Sailing Log Book

DATE

WEATHER

WIND

SEA CONDITIONS

DESTINATION

FORECAST

VISIBILITY

ETA

TIME	COURSE	SPEED	DISTANCE	NAVIGATION NOTES	REMARKS

EVENTS / OBSERVATIONS

....

....

....

....

....

....

....

TIME COMPLETED

AVERAGE SPEED

DAYS RUN

FUEL ON BOARD

CREW & GUESTS

....

....

....

....

....

CAPTAIN

Sailing Log Book

DATE _____   DESTINATION _____

WEATHER _____   FORECAST _____

WIND _____   VISIBILITY _____

SEA CONDITIONS _____   ETA _____

TIME	COURSE	SPEED	DISTANCE	NAVIGATION NOTES	REMARKS

EVENTS / OBSERVATIONS

....
....
....
....
....
....
....

TIME COMPLETED _____   DAYS RUN _____

AVERAGE SPEED _____   FUEL ON BOARD _____

CREW & GUESTS

....
....
....
....
....

CAPTAIN _____

Sailing Log Book ⚓

DATE

WEATHER

WIND

SEA CONDITIONS

DESTINATION

FORECAST

VISIBILITY

ETA

TIME	COURSE	SPEED	DISTANCE	NAVIGATION NOTES	REMARKS

EVENTS / OBSERVATIONS

....
....
....
....
....
....
....

TIME COMPLETED

AVERAGE SPEED

DAYS RUN

FUEL ON BOARD

CREW & GUESTS

....
....
....
....
....

CAPTAIN

Sailing Log Book

DATE		DESTINATION	
WEATHER		FORECAST	
WIND		VISIBILITY	
SEA CONDITIONS		ETA	

TIME	COURSE	SPEED	DISTANCE	NAVIGATION NOTES	REMARKS

EVENTS / OBSERVATIONS

| TIME COMPLETED | | DAYS RUN | |
| AVERAGE SPEED | | FUEL ON BOARD | |

CREW & GUESTS

CAPTAIN

Sailing Log Book

DATE _____   DESTINATION _____

WEATHER _____   FORECAST _____

WIND _____   VISIBILITY _____

SEA CONDITIONS _____   ETA _____

TIME	COURSE	SPEED	DISTANCE	NAVIGATION NOTES	REMARKS

EVENTS / OBSERVATIONS

....
....
....
....
....
....
....

TIME COMPLETED _____   DAYS RUN _____

AVERAGE SPEED _____   FUEL ON BOARD _____

CREW & GUESTS

....
....
....
....

CAPTAIN _____

Sailing Log Book

DATE

WEATHER

WIND

SEA CONDITIONS

DESTINATION

FORECAST

VISIBILITY

ETA

TIME	COURSE	SPEED	DISTANCE	NAVIGATION NOTES	REMARKS

EVENTS / OBSERVATIONS

TIME COMPLETED

AVERAGE SPEED

DAYS RUN

FUEL ON BOARD

CREW & GUESTS

CAPTAIN

Sailing Log Book ☸

DATE   DESTINATION

WEATHER   FORECAST

WIND   VISIBILITY

SEA CONDITIONS   ETA

TIME	COURSE	SPEED	DISTANCE	NAVIGATION NOTES	REMARKS

EVENTS / OBSERVATIONS

....
....
....
....
....
....
....

TIME COMPLETED   DAYS RUN

AVERAGE SPEED   FUEL ON BOARD

CREW & GUESTS

....
....
....
....

CAPTAIN

Sailing Log Book

DATE		DESTINATION	
WEATHER		FORECAST	
WIND		VISIBILITY	
SEA CONDITIONS		ETA	

TIME	COURSE	SPEED	DISTANCE	NAVIGATION NOTES	REMARKS

EVENTS / OBSERVATIONS

....
....
....
....
....
....
....

| TIME COMPLETED | | DAYS RUN | |
| AVERAGE SPEED | | FUEL ON BOARD | |

CREW & GUESTS

....
....
....
....

CAPTAIN

Sailing Log Book

DATE

WEATHER

WIND

SEA CONDITIONS

DESTINATION

FORECAST

VISIBILITY

ETA

TIME	COURSE	SPEED	DISTANCE	NAVIGATION NOTES	REMARKS

EVENTS / OBSERVATIONS

....
....
....
....
....
....
....

TIME COMPLETED

AVERAGE SPEED

DAYS RUN

FUEL ON BOARD

CREW & GUESTS

....
....
....
....

CAPTAIN

Sailing Log Book ☸

DATE _____   DESTINATION _____

WEATHER _____   FORECAST _____

WIND _____   VISIBILITY _____

SEA CONDITIONS _____   ETA _____

TIME	COURSE	SPEED	DISTANCE	NAVIGATION NOTES	REMARKS

EVENTS / OBSERVATIONS

....
....
....
....
....
....
....

TIME COMPLETED _____   DAYS RUN _____

AVERAGE SPEED _____   FUEL ON BOARD _____

CREW & GUESTS

....
....
....
....

CAPTAIN _____

Sailing Log Book

DATE   DESTINATION

WEATHER   FORECAST

WIND   VISIBILITY

SEA CONDITIONS   ETA

TIME	COURSE	SPEED	DISTANCE	NAVIGATION NOTES	REMARKS

EVENTS / OBSERVATIONS

....
....
....
....
....
....

TIME COMPLETED   DAYS RUN

AVERAGE SPEED   FUEL ON BOARD

CREW & GUESTS

....
....
....
....

CAPTAIN

Sailing Log Book ⎈

DATE		DESTINATION	
WEATHER		FORECAST	
WIND		VISIBILITY	
SEA CONDITIONS		ETA	

TIME	COURSE	SPEED	DISTANCE	NAVIGATION NOTES	REMARKS

EVENTS / OBSERVATIONS

....
....
....
....
....
....
....

TIME COMPLETED		DAYS RUN	
AVERAGE SPEED		FUEL ON BOARD	

CREW & GUESTS

....
....
....
....

CAPTAIN

Sailing Log Book

DATE

WEATHER

WIND

SEA CONDITIONS

DESTINATION

FORECAST

VISIBILITY

ETA

TIME	COURSE	SPEED	DISTANCE	NAVIGATION NOTES	REMARKS

EVENTS / OBSERVATIONS

....
....
....
....
....
....
....

TIME COMPLETED

AVERAGE SPEED

DAYS RUN

FUEL ON BOARD

CREW & GUESTS

....
....
....
....

CAPTAIN

Sailing Log Book

DATE   **DESTINATION**

WEATHER   **FORECAST**

WIND   **VISIBILITY**

SEA CONDITIONS   **ETA**

TIME	COURSE	SPEED	DISTANCE	NAVIGATION NOTES	REMARKS

EVENTS / OBSERVATIONS

....
....
....
....
....
....
....

TIME COMPLETED   **DAYS RUN**

AVERAGE SPEED   **FUEL ON BOARD**

CREW & GUESTS

....
....
....
....

CAPTAIN

Sailing Log Book

DATE	**DESTINATION**
WEATHER	**FORECAST**
WIND	**VISIBILITY**
SEA CONDITIONS	**ETA**

TIME	COURSE	SPEED	DISTANCE	NAVIGATION NOTES	REMARKS

EVENTS / OBSERVATIONS

....
....
....
....
....
....
....

TIME COMPLETED	**DAYS RUN**
AVERAGE SPEED	**FUEL ON BOARD**

CREW & GUESTS

....
....
....
....

CAPTAIN

Sailing Log Book

DATE _____   DESTINATION _____

WEATHER _____   FORECAST _____

WIND _____   VISIBILITY _____

SEA CONDITIONS _____   ETA _____

TIME	COURSE	SPEED	DISTANCE	NAVIGATION NOTES	REMARKS

EVENTS / OBSERVATIONS

....
....
....
....
....
....
....

TIME COMPLETED _____   DAYS RUN _____

AVERAGE SPEED _____   FUEL ON BOARD _____

CREW & GUESTS

....
....
....
....

CAPTAIN _____

Sailing Log Book

DATE

DESTINATION

WEATHER

FORECAST

WIND

VISIBILITY

SEA CONDITIONS

ETA

TIME	COURSE	SPEED	DISTANCE	NAVIGATION NOTES	REMARKS

EVENTS / OBSERVATIONS

....
....
....
....
....
....
....

TIME COMPLETED

DAYS RUN

AVERAGE SPEED

FUEL ON BOARD

CREW & GUESTS

....
....
....
....

CAPTAIN

Sailing Log Book

DATE _____ DESTINATION _____

WEATHER _____ FORECAST _____

WIND _____ VISIBILITY _____

SEA CONDITIONS _____ ETA _____

TIME	COURSE	SPEED	DISTANCE	NAVIGATION NOTES	REMARKS

EVENTS / OBSERVATIONS

....
....
....
....
....
....
....

TIME COMPLETED _____ DAYS RUN _____

AVERAGE SPEED _____ FUEL ON BOARD _____

CREW & GUESTS

....
....
....
....

CAPTAIN _____

Sailing Log Book ☸

DATE

WEATHER

WIND

SEA CONDITIONS

DESTINATION

FORECAST

VISIBILITY

ETA

TIME	COURSE	SPEED	DISTANCE	NAVIGATION NOTES	REMARKS

EVENTS / OBSERVATIONS

....
....
....
....
....
....
....

TIME COMPLETED

AVERAGE SPEED

DAYS RUN

FUEL ON BOARD

CREW & GUESTS

....
....
....
....

CAPTAIN

Sailing Log Book ⚓

DATE		DESTINATION	
WEATHER		FORECAST	
WIND		VISIBILITY	
SEA CONDITIONS		ETA	

TIME	COURSE	SPEED	DISTANCE	NAVIGATION NOTES	REMARKS

EVENTS / OBSERVATIONS

....
....
....
....
....
....
....

TIME COMPLETED		DAYS RUN	
AVERAGE SPEED		FUEL ON BOARD	

CREW & GUESTS

....
....
....
....

CAPTAIN

Sailing Log Book

DATE _____ DESTINATION _____

WEATHER _____ FORECAST _____

WIND _____ VISIBILITY _____

SEA CONDITIONS _____ ETA _____

TIME	COURSE	SPEED	DISTANCE	NAVIGATION NOTES	REMARKS

EVENTS / OBSERVATIONS

....
....
....
....
....
....
....

TIME COMPLETED _____ DAYS RUN _____

AVERAGE SPEED _____ FUEL ON BOARD _____

CREW & GUESTS

....
....
....
....

CAPTAIN _____

Sailing Log Book

DATE		DESTINATION	
WEATHER		FORECAST	
WIND		VISIBILITY	
SEA CONDITIONS		ETA	

TIME	COURSE	SPEED	DISTANCE	NAVIGATION NOTES	REMARKS

EVENTS / OBSERVATIONS

TIME COMPLETED   DAYS RUN

AVERAGE SPEED   FUEL ON BOARD

CREW & GUESTS

CAPTAIN

Sailing Log Book ☸

DATE   DESTINATION

WEATHER   FORECAST

WIND   VISIBILITY

SEA CONDITIONS   ETA

TIME	COURSE	SPEED	DISTANCE	NAVIGATION NOTES	REMARKS

EVENTS / OBSERVATIONS

....
....
....
....
....
....
....

TIME COMPLETED   DAYS RUN

AVERAGE SPEED   FUEL ON BOARD

CREW & GUESTS

....
....
....
....

CAPTAIN

Sailing Log Book ☸

DATE _____ DESTINATION _____

WEATHER _____ FORECAST _____

WIND _____ VISIBILITY _____

SEA CONDITIONS _____ ETA _____

TIME	COURSE	SPEED	DISTANCE	NAVIGATION NOTES	REMARKS

EVENTS / OBSERVATIONS

....
....
....
....
....
....
....

TIME COMPLETED _____ DAYS RUN _____

AVERAGE SPEED _____ FUEL ON BOARD _____

CREW & GUESTS

....
....
....
....

CAPTAIN _____

Sailing Log Book ☸

DATE   **DESTINATION**

WEATHER   **FORECAST**

WIND   **VISIBILITY**

SEA CONDITIONS   **ETA**

TIME	COURSE	SPEED	DISTANCE	NAVIGATION NOTES	REMARKS

EVENTS / OBSERVATIONS

....
....
....
....
....
....
....

TIME COMPLETED   **DAYS RUN**

AVERAGE SPEED   **FUEL ON BOARD**

CREW & GUESTS

....
....
....
....

CAPTAIN

Sailing Log Book

DATE		DESTINATION	
WEATHER		FORECAST	
WIND		VISIBILITY	
SEA CONDITIONS		ETA	

TIME	COURSE	SPEED	DISTANCE	NAVIGATION NOTES	REMARKS

EVENTS / OBSERVATIONS

....
....
....
....
....
....
....

TIME COMPLETED		DAYS RUN	
AVERAGE SPEED		FUEL ON BOARD	

CREW & GUESTS

....
....
....
....

CAPTAIN

Sailing Log Book

DATE   DESTINATION

WEATHER   FORECAST

WIND   VISIBILITY

SEA CONDITIONS   ETA

TIME	COURSE	SPEED	DISTANCE	NAVIGATION NOTES	REMARKS

EVENTS / OBSERVATIONS

....
....
....
....
....
....
....

TIME COMPLETED   DAYS RUN

AVERAGE SPEED   FUEL ON BOARD

CREW & GUESTS

....
....
....
....

CAPTAIN

Sailing Log Book

DATE _____ DESTINATION _____

WEATHER _____ FORECAST _____

WIND _____ VISIBILITY _____

SEA CONDITIONS _____ ETA _____

TIME	COURSE	SPEED	DISTANCE	NAVIGATION NOTES	REMARKS

EVENTS / OBSERVATIONS

....
....
....
....
....
....
....

TIME COMPLETED _____ DAYS RUN _____

AVERAGE SPEED _____ FUEL ON BOARD _____

CREW & GUESTS

....
....
....
....

CAPTAIN _____

Sailing Log Book ☸

DATE   **DESTINATION**

WEATHER   **FORECAST**

WIND   **VISIBILITY**

SEA CONDITIONS   **ETA**

TIME	COURSE	SPEED	DISTANCE	NAVIGATION NOTES	REMARKS

EVENTS / OBSERVATIONS

....
....
....
....
....
....
....

TIME COMPLETED   **DAYS RUN**

AVERAGE SPEED   **FUEL ON BOARD**

CREW & GUESTS

....
....
....
....

CAPTAIN

Sailing Log Book

DATE _____   DESTINATION _____

WEATHER _____   FORECAST _____

WIND _____   VISIBILITY _____

SEA CONDITIONS _____   ETA _____

TIME	COURSE	SPEED	DISTANCE	NAVIGATION NOTES	REMARKS

EVENTS / OBSERVATIONS

....
....
....
....
....
....
....

TIME COMPLETED _____   DAYS RUN _____

AVERAGE SPEED _____   FUEL ON BOARD _____

CREW & GUESTS

....
....
....
....

CAPTAIN _____

Sailing Log Book

DATE

DESTINATION

WEATHER

FORECAST

WIND

VISIBILITY

SEA CONDITIONS

ETA

TIME	COURSE	SPEED	DISTANCE	NAVIGATION NOTES	REMARKS

EVENTS / OBSERVATIONS

....
....
....
....
....
....
....

TIME COMPLETED

DAYS RUN

AVERAGE SPEED

FUEL ON BOARD

CREW & GUESTS

....
....
....
....

CAPTAIN

Sailing Log Book ☸

DATE		DESTINATION	
WEATHER		FORECAST	
WIND		VISIBILITY	
SEA CONDITIONS		ETA	

TIME	COURSE	SPEED	DISTANCE	NAVIGATION NOTES	REMARKS

EVENTS / OBSERVATIONS

....
....
....
....
....
....
....

TIME COMPLETED		DAYS RUN	
AVERAGE SPEED		FUEL ON BOARD	

CREW & GUESTS

....
....
....
....

CAPTAIN

Sailing Log Book ⚓

DATE _____   DESTINATION _____

WEATHER _____   FORECAST _____

WIND _____   VISIBILITY _____

SEA CONDITIONS _____   ETA _____

TIME	COURSE	SPEED	DISTANCE	NAVIGATION NOTES	REMARKS

EVENTS / OBSERVATIONS

....
....
....
....
....
....
....

TIME COMPLETED _____   DAYS RUN _____

AVERAGE SPEED _____   FUEL ON BOARD _____

CREW & GUESTS

....
....
....
....

CAPTAIN _____

Sailing Log Book ☸

DATE   **DESTINATION**

WEATHER   **FORECAST**

WIND   **VISIBILITY**

SEA CONDITIONS   **ETA**

TIME	COURSE	SPEED	DISTANCE	NAVIGATION NOTES	REMARKS

EVENTS / OBSERVATIONS

....
....
....
....
....
....
....

TIME COMPLETED   **DAYS RUN**

AVERAGE SPEED   **FUEL ON BOARD**

CREW & GUESTS

....
....
....
....

CAPTAIN

Sailing Log Book

DATE

DESTINATION

WEATHER

FORECAST

WIND

VISIBILITY

SEA CONDITIONS

ETA

TIME	COURSE	SPEED	DISTANCE	NAVIGATION NOTES	REMARKS

EVENTS / OBSERVATIONS

....

....

....

....

....

....

....

TIME COMPLETED

DAYS RUN

AVERAGE SPEED

FUEL ON BOARD

CREW & GUESTS

....

....

....

....

CAPTAIN

Sailing Log Book ☸

DATE _____   DESTINATION _____

WEATHER _____   FORECAST _____

WIND _____   VISIBILITY _____

SEA CONDITIONS _____   ETA _____

TIME	COURSE	SPEED	DISTANCE	NAVIGATION NOTES	REMARKS

EVENTS / OBSERVATIONS

....
....
....
....
....
....
....

TIME COMPLETED _____   DAYS RUN _____

AVERAGE SPEED _____   FUEL ON BOARD _____

CREW & GUESTS

....
....
....
....

CAPTAIN _____

Sailing Log Book

DATE		DESTINATION	
WEATHER		FORECAST	
WIND		VISIBILITY	
SEA CONDITIONS		ETA	

TIME	COURSE	SPEED	DISTANCE	NAVIGATION NOTES	REMARKS

EVENTS / OBSERVATIONS

....
....
....
....
....
....
....

TIME COMPLETED		DAYS RUN	
AVERAGE SPEED		FUEL ON BOARD	

CREW & GUESTS

....
....
....
....

CAPTAIN

Sailing Log Book

DATE		DESTINATION	
WEATHER		FORECAST	
WIND		VISIBILITY	
SEA CONDITIONS		ETA	

TIME	COURSE	SPEED	DISTANCE	NAVIGATION NOTES	REMARKS

EVENTS / OBSERVATIONS

....
....
....
....
....
....
....

TIME COMPLETED		DAYS RUN	
AVERAGE SPEED		FUEL ON BOARD	

CREW & GUESTS

....
....
....
....

CAPTAIN

Sailing Log Book ☸

DATE   DESTINATION

WEATHER   FORECAST

WIND   VISIBILITY

SEA CONDITIONS   ETA

TIME	COURSE	SPEED	DISTANCE	NAVIGATION NOTES	REMARKS

EVENTS / OBSERVATIONS

....
....
....
....
....
....
....

TIME COMPLETED   DAYS RUN

AVERAGE SPEED   FUEL ON BOARD

CREW & GUESTS

....
....
....
....

CAPTAIN

Sailing Log Book ☸

DATE _____   **DESTINATION** _____

WEATHER _____   **FORECAST** _____

WIND _____   **VISIBILITY** _____

SEA CONDITIONS _____   **ETA** _____

TIME	COURSE	SPEED	DISTANCE	NAVIGATION NOTES	REMARKS

EVENTS / OBSERVATIONS

....
....
....
....
....
....
....

TIME COMPLETED _____   **DAYS RUN** _____

AVERAGE SPEED _____   **FUEL ON BOARD** _____

CREW & GUESTS

....
....
....
....

CAPTAIN _____

Sailing Log Book

DATE

WEATHER

WIND

SEA CONDITIONS

DESTINATION

FORECAST

VISIBILITY

ETA

TIME	COURSE	SPEED	DISTANCE	NAVIGATION NOTES	REMARKS

EVENTS / OBSERVATIONS

....
....
....
....
....
....
....

TIME COMPLETED

AVERAGE SPEED

DAYS RUN

FUEL ON BOARD

CREW & GUESTS

....
....
....
....

CAPTAIN

Sailing Log Book

DATE		DESTINATION	
WEATHER		FORECAST	
WIND		VISIBILITY	
SEA CONDITIONS		ETA	

TIME	COURSE	SPEED	DISTANCE	NAVIGATION NOTES	REMARKS

EVENTS / OBSERVATIONS

....
....
....
....
....
....
....

| TIME COMPLETED | | DAYS RUN | |
| AVERAGE SPEED | | FUEL ON BOARD | |

CREW & GUESTS

....
....
....
....

CAPTAIN

Sailing Log Book

DATE

DESTINATION

WEATHER

FORECAST

WIND

VISIBILITY

SEA CONDITIONS

ETA

TIME	COURSE	SPEED	DISTANCE	NAVIGATION NOTES	REMARKS

EVENTS / OBSERVATIONS

....
....
....
....
....
....
....

TIME COMPLETED

DAYS RUN

AVERAGE SPEED

FUEL ON BOARD

CREW & GUESTS

....
....
....
....

CAPTAIN

Sailing Log Book

DATE _____   DESTINATION _____

WEATHER _____   FORECAST _____

WIND _____   VISIBILITY _____

SEA CONDITIONS _____   ETA _____

TIME	COURSE	SPEED	DISTANCE	NAVIGATION NOTES	REMARKS

EVENTS / OBSERVATIONS

....
....
....
....
....
....
....

TIME COMPLETED _____   DAYS RUN _____

AVERAGE SPEED _____   FUEL ON BOARD _____

CREW & GUESTS

....
....
....
....

CAPTAIN _____

Sailing Log Book

DATE

WEATHER

WIND

SEA CONDITIONS

DESTINATION

FORECAST

VISIBILITY

ETA

TIME	COURSE	SPEED	DISTANCE	NAVIGATION NOTES	REMARKS

EVENTS / OBSERVATIONS

....
....
....
....
....
....
....

TIME COMPLETED

AVERAGE SPEED

DAYS RUN

FUEL ON BOARD

CREW & GUESTS

....
....
....
....

CAPTAIN

Sailing Log Book ☸

DATE	**DESTINATION**	
WEATHER	**FORECAST**	
WIND	**VISIBILITY**	
SEA CONDITIONS	**ETA**	

TIME	COURSE	SPEED	DISTANCE	NAVIGATION NOTES	REMARKS

EVENTS / OBSERVATIONS

....
....
....
....
....
....
....

TIME COMPLETED	**DAYS RUN**
AVERAGE SPEED	**FUEL ON BOARD**

CREW & GUESTS

....
....
....
....

CAPTAIN

Sailing Log Book ☸

DATE   DESTINATION

WEATHER   FORECAST

WIND   VISIBILITY

SEA CONDITIONS   ETA

TIME	COURSE	SPEED	DISTANCE	NAVIGATION NOTES	REMARKS

EVENTS / OBSERVATIONS

....
....
....
....
....
....
....

TIME COMPLETED   DAYS RUN

AVERAGE SPEED   FUEL ON BOARD

CREW & GUESTS

....
....
....
....
....

CAPTAIN

Sailing Log Book ☸

DATE			**DESTINATION**		
WEATHER			**FORECAST**		
WIND			**VISIBILITY**		
SEA CONDITIONS			**ETA**		

TIME	COURSE	SPEED	DISTANCE	NAVIGATION NOTES	REMARKS

EVENTS / OBSERVATIONS

....
....
....
....
....
....
....

TIME COMPLETED   **DAYS RUN**

AVERAGE SPEED   **FUEL ON BOARD**

CREW & GUESTS

....
....
....
....

CAPTAIN

Sailing Log Book

DATE

WEATHER

WIND

SEA CONDITIONS

DESTINATION

FORECAST

VISIBILITY

ETA

TIME	COURSE	SPEED	DISTANCE	NAVIGATION NOTES	REMARKS

EVENTS / OBSERVATIONS

....
....
....
....
....
....
....

TIME COMPLETED

AVERAGE SPEED

DAYS RUN

FUEL ON BOARD

CREW & GUESTS

....
....
....
....

CAPTAIN

Sailing Log Book

DATE		DESTINATION	
WEATHER		FORECAST	
WIND		VISIBILITY	
SEA CONDITIONS		ETA	

TIME	COURSE	SPEED	DISTANCE	NAVIGATION NOTES	REMARKS

EVENTS / OBSERVATIONS

| TIME COMPLETED | | DAYS RUN | |
| AVERAGE SPEED | | FUEL ON BOARD | |

CREW & GUESTS

CAPTAIN

Sailing Log Book ☸

DATE   DESTINATION

WEATHER   FORECAST

WIND   VISIBILITY

SEA CONDITIONS   ETA

TIME	COURSE	SPEED	DISTANCE	NAVIGATION NOTES	REMARKS

EVENTS / OBSERVATIONS

....

....

....

....

....

....

....

TIME COMPLETED   DAYS RUN

AVERAGE SPEED   FUEL ON BOARD

CREW & GUESTS

....

....

....

....

CAPTAIN

Sailing Log Book ⚓

DATE   **DESTINATION**

WEATHER   **FORECAST**

WIND   **VISIBILITY**

SEA CONDITIONS   **ETA**

TIME	COURSE	SPEED	DISTANCE	NAVIGATION NOTES	REMARKS

EVENTS / OBSERVATIONS

....
....
....
....
....
....
....

TIME COMPLETED   **DAYS RUN**

AVERAGE SPEED   **FUEL ON BOARD**

CREW & GUESTS

....
....
....
....

CAPTAIN

Sailing Log Book

DATE

DESTINATION

WEATHER

FORECAST

WIND

VISIBILITY

SEA CONDITIONS

ETA

TIME	COURSE	SPEED	DISTANCE	NAVIGATION NOTES	REMARKS

EVENTS / OBSERVATIONS

....
....
....
....
....
....

TIME COMPLETED

DAYS RUN

AVERAGE SPEED

FUEL ON BOARD

CREW & GUESTS

....
....
....
....

CAPTAIN

Sailing Log Book ☸

DATE		DESTINATION	
WEATHER		FORECAST	
WIND		VISIBILITY	
SEA CONDITIONS		ETA	

TIME	COURSE	SPEED	DISTANCE	NAVIGATION NOTES	REMARKS

EVENTS / OBSERVATIONS

....
....
....
....
....
....
....

| TIME COMPLETED | | DAYS RUN | |
| AVERAGE SPEED | | FUEL ON BOARD | |

CREW & GUESTS

....
....
....
....

CAPTAIN

Sailing Log Book ☸

DATE   **DESTINATION**

WEATHER   **FORECAST**

WIND   **VISIBILITY**

SEA CONDITIONS   **ETA**

TIME	COURSE	SPEED	DISTANCE	NAVIGATION NOTES	REMARKS

EVENTS / OBSERVATIONS

....
....
....
....
....
....
....

TIME COMPLETED   **DAYS RUN**

AVERAGE SPEED   **FUEL ON BOARD**

CREW & GUESTS

....
....
....
....

CAPTAIN

Sailing Log Book

DATE		DESTINATION	
WEATHER		FORECAST	
WIND		VISIBILITY	
SEA CONDITIONS		ETA	

TIME	COURSE	SPEED	DISTANCE	NAVIGATION NOTES	REMARKS

EVENTS / OBSERVATIONS

....
....
....
....
....
....
....

TIME COMPLETED		DAYS RUN	
AVERAGE SPEED		FUEL ON BOARD	

CREW & GUESTS

....
....
....
....

CAPTAIN

Sailing Log Book ☸

DATE   DESTINATION

WEATHER   FORECAST

WIND   VISIBILITY

SEA CONDITIONS   ETA

TIME	COURSE	SPEED	DISTANCE	NAVIGATION NOTES	REMARKS

EVENTS / OBSERVATIONS

....
....
....
....
....
....
....

TIME COMPLETED   DAYS RUN

AVERAGE SPEED   FUEL ON BOARD

CREW & GUESTS

....
....
....
....

CAPTAIN

Sailing Log Book

DATE _____ DESTINATION _____

WEATHER _____ FORECAST _____

WIND _____ VISIBILITY _____

SEA CONDITIONS _____ ETA _____

TIME	COURSE	SPEED	DISTANCE	NAVIGATION NOTES	REMARKS

EVENTS / OBSERVATIONS

TIME COMPLETED _____ DAYS RUN _____

AVERAGE SPEED _____ FUEL ON BOARD _____

CREW & GUESTS

CAPTAIN _____

Sailing Log Book

DATE

DESTINATION

WEATHER

FORECAST

WIND

VISIBILITY

SEA CONDITIONS

ETA

TIME	COURSE	SPEED	DISTANCE	NAVIGATION NOTES	REMARKS

EVENTS / OBSERVATIONS

....
....
....
....
....
....
....

TIME COMPLETED

DAYS RUN

AVERAGE SPEED

FUEL ON BOARD

CREW & GUESTS

....
....
....
....

CAPTAIN

Sailing Log Book

DATE _____   DESTINATION _____

WEATHER _____   FORECAST _____

WIND _____   VISIBILITY _____

SEA CONDITIONS _____   ETA _____

TIME	COURSE	SPEED	DISTANCE	NAVIGATION NOTES	REMARKS

EVENTS / OBSERVATIONS

....
....
....
....
....
....
....

TIME COMPLETED _____   DAYS RUN _____

AVERAGE SPEED _____   FUEL ON BOARD _____

CREW & GUESTS

....
....
....
....

CAPTAIN _____

Sailing Log Book

DATE

WEATHER

WIND

SEA CONDITIONS

DESTINATION

FORECAST

VISIBILITY

ETA

TIME	COURSE	SPEED	DISTANCE	NAVIGATION NOTES	REMARKS

EVENTS / OBSERVATIONS

....
....
....
....
....
....
....

TIME COMPLETED

AVERAGE SPEED

DAYS RUN

FUEL ON BOARD

CREW & GUESTS

....
....
....
....

CAPTAIN

Sailing Log Book

DATE _____ DESTINATION _____

WEATHER _____ FORECAST _____

WIND _____ VISIBILITY _____

SEA CONDITIONS _____ ETA _____

TIME	COURSE	SPEED	DISTANCE	NAVIGATION NOTES	REMARKS

EVENTS / OBSERVATIONS

....
....
....
....
....
....
....

TIME COMPLETED _____ DAYS RUN _____

AVERAGE SPEED _____ FUEL ON BOARD _____

CREW & GUESTS

....
....
....
....

CAPTAIN _____

Sailing Log Book

DATE   DESTINATION

WEATHER   FORECAST

WIND   VISIBILITY

SEA CONDITIONS   ETA

TIME	COURSE	SPEED	DISTANCE	NAVIGATION NOTES	REMARKS

EVENTS / OBSERVATIONS

....
....
....
....
....
....
....

TIME COMPLETED   DAYS RUN

AVERAGE SPEED   FUEL ON BOARD

CREW & GUESTS

....
....
....
....

CAPTAIN

Sailing Log Book ☸

DATE

WEATHER

WIND

SEA CONDITIONS

DESTINATION

FORECAST

VISIBILITY

ETA

TIME	COURSE	SPEED	DISTANCE	NAVIGATION NOTES	REMARKS

EVENTS / OBSERVATIONS

....
....
....
....
....
....
....

TIME COMPLETED

AVERAGE SPEED

DAYS RUN

FUEL ON BOARD

CREW & GUESTS

....
....
....
....

CAPTAIN

Sailing Log Book ☸

DATE

DESTINATION

WEATHER

FORECAST

WIND

VISIBILITY

SEA CONDITIONS

ETA

TIME	COURSE	SPEED	DISTANCE	NAVIGATION NOTES	REMARKS

EVENTS / OBSERVATIONS

....

....

....

....

....

....

TIME COMPLETED

DAYS RUN

AVERAGE SPEED

FUEL ON BOARD

CREW & GUESTS

....

....

....

....

CAPTAIN

Sailing Log Book

DATE		DESTINATION	
WEATHER		FORECAST	
WIND		VISIBILITY	
SEA CONDITIONS		ETA	

TIME	COURSE	SPEED	DISTANCE	NAVIGATION NOTES	REMARKS

EVENTS / OBSERVATIONS

....
....
....
....
....
....
....

| TIME COMPLETED | | DAYS RUN | |
| AVERAGE SPEED | | FUEL ON BOARD | |

CREW & GUESTS

....
....
....
....

CAPTAIN

Sailing Log Book

DATE

WEATHER

WIND

SEA CONDITIONS

DESTINATION

FORECAST

VISIBILITY

ETA

TIME	COURSE	SPEED	DISTANCE	NAVIGATION NOTES	REMARKS

EVENTS / OBSERVATIONS

TIME COMPLETED

AVERAGE SPEED

DAYS RUN

FUEL ON BOARD

CREW & GUESTS

CAPTAIN

Sailing Log Book

DATE		DESTINATION	
WEATHER		FORECAST	
WIND		VISIBILITY	
SEA CONDITIONS		ETA	

TIME	COURSE	SPEED	DISTANCE	NAVIGATION NOTES	REMARKS

EVENTS / OBSERVATIONS

....
....
....
....
....
....
....

TIME COMPLETED

AVERAGE SPEED

DAYS RUN

FUEL ON BOARD

CREW & GUESTS

....
....
....
....

CAPTAIN

Sailing Log Book

DATE   DESTINATION

WEATHER   FORECAST

WIND   VISIBILITY

SEA CONDITIONS   ETA

TIME	COURSE	SPEED	DISTANCE	NAVIGATION NOTES	REMARKS

EVENTS / OBSERVATIONS

TIME COMPLETED   DAYS RUN

AVERAGE SPEED   FUEL ON BOARD

CREW & GUESTS

CAPTAIN

Sailing Log Book ⚓

DATE		DESTINATION	
WEATHER		FORECAST	
WIND		VISIBILITY	
SEA CONDITIONS		ETA	

TIME	COURSE	SPEED	DISTANCE	NAVIGATION NOTES	REMARKS

EVENTS / OBSERVATIONS

....
....
....
....
....
....
....

| TIME COMPLETED | | DAYS RUN | |
| AVERAGE SPEED | | FUEL ON BOARD | |

CREW & GUESTS

....
....
....
....

CAPTAIN

Sailing Log Book

DATE

DESTINATION

WEATHER

FORECAST

WIND

VISIBILITY

SEA CONDITIONS

ETA

TIME	COURSE	SPEED	DISTANCE	NAVIGATION NOTES	REMARKS

EVENTS / OBSERVATIONS

....
....
....
....
....
....
....

TIME COMPLETED

DAYS RUN

AVERAGE SPEED

FUEL ON BOARD

CREW & GUESTS

....
....
....
....

CAPTAIN

Sailing Log Book

DATE		DESTINATION	
WEATHER		FORECAST	
WIND		VISIBILITY	
SEA CONDITIONS		ETA	

TIME	COURSE	SPEED	DISTANCE	NAVIGATION NOTES	REMARKS

EVENTS / OBSERVATIONS

TIME COMPLETED _____ DAYS RUN _____

AVERAGE SPEED _____ FUEL ON BOARD _____

CREW & GUESTS

CAPTAIN _____

Sailing Log Book ☸

DATE

WEATHER

WIND

SEA CONDITIONS

DESTINATION

FORECAST

VISIBILITY

ETA

TIME	COURSE	SPEED	DISTANCE	NAVIGATION NOTES	REMARKS

EVENTS / OBSERVATIONS

....
....
....
....
....
....
....

TIME COMPLETED

AVERAGE SPEED

DAYS RUN

FUEL ON BOARD

CREW & GUESTS

....
....
....
....

CAPTAIN

Sailing Log Book

DATE _____ DESTINATION _____

WEATHER _____ FORECAST _____

WIND _____ VISIBILITY _____

SEA CONDITIONS _____ ETA _____

TIME	COURSE	SPEED	DISTANCE	NAVIGATION NOTES	REMARKS

EVENTS / OBSERVATIONS

....
....
....
....
....
....
....

TIME COMPLETED _____ DAYS RUN _____

AVERAGE SPEED _____ FUEL ON BOARD _____

CREW & GUESTS

....
....
....
....

CAPTAIN _____

Sailing Log Book ⚓

DATE

DESTINATION

WEATHER

FORECAST

WIND

VISIBILITY

SEA CONDITIONS

ETA

TIME	COURSE	SPEED	DISTANCE	NAVIGATION NOTES	REMARKS

EVENTS / OBSERVATIONS

....
....
....
....
....
....
....

TIME COMPLETED

DAYS RUN

AVERAGE SPEED

FUEL ON BOARD

CREW & GUESTS

....
....
....
....

CAPTAIN

Sailing Log Book ⚓

DATE		DESTINATION	
WEATHER		FORECAST	
WIND		VISIBILITY	
SEA CONDITIONS		ETA	

TIME	COURSE	SPEED	DISTANCE	NAVIGATION NOTES	REMARKS

EVENTS / OBSERVATIONS

....
....
....
....
....
....
....

| TIME COMPLETED | | DAYS RUN | |
| AVERAGE SPEED | | FUEL ON BOARD | |

CREW & GUESTS

....
....
....
....

CAPTAIN

Sailing Log Book

DATE

WEATHER

WIND

SEA CONDITIONS

DESTINATION

FORECAST

VISIBILITY

ETA

TIME	COURSE	SPEED	DISTANCE	NAVIGATION NOTES	REMARKS

EVENTS / OBSERVATIONS

....
....
....
....
....
....
....

TIME COMPLETED

AVERAGE SPEED

DAYS RUN

FUEL ON BOARD

CREW & GUESTS

....
....
....
....

CAPTAIN

Sailing Log Book

DATE _____   DESTINATION _____

WEATHER _____   FORECAST _____

WIND _____   VISIBILITY _____

SEA CONDITIONS _____   ETA _____

TIME	COURSE	SPEED	DISTANCE	NAVIGATION NOTES	REMARKS

EVENTS / OBSERVATIONS

....
....
....
....
....
....
....

TIME COMPLETED _____   DAYS RUN _____

AVERAGE SPEED _____   FUEL ON BOARD _____

CREW & GUESTS

....
....
....
....

CAPTAIN _____

Sailing Log Book ☸

DATE   **DESTINATION**

WEATHER   **FORECAST**

WIND   **VISIBILITY**

SEA CONDITIONS   **ETA**

TIME	COURSE	SPEED	DISTANCE	NAVIGATION NOTES	REMARKS

EVENTS / OBSERVATIONS

....
....
....
....
....
....

TIME COMPLETED   **DAYS RUN**

AVERAGE SPEED   **FUEL ON BOARD**

CREW & GUESTS

....
....
....
....

CAPTAIN

Sailing Log Book

DATE		DESTINATION	
WEATHER		FORECAST	
WIND		VISIBILITY	
SEA CONDITIONS		ETA	

TIME	COURSE	SPEED	DISTANCE	NAVIGATION NOTES	REMARKS

EVENTS / OBSERVATIONS

TIME COMPLETED _____   DAYS RUN _____

AVERAGE SPEED _____   FUEL ON BOARD _____

CREW & GUESTS

CAPTAIN _____

Sailing Log Book ☸

DATE

WEATHER

WIND

SEA CONDITIONS

DESTINATION

FORECAST

VISIBILITY

ETA

TIME	COURSE	SPEED	DISTANCE	NAVIGATION NOTES	REMARKS

EVENTS / OBSERVATIONS

....
....
....
....
....
....
....

TIME COMPLETED

AVERAGE SPEED

DAYS RUN

FUEL ON BOARD

CREW & GUESTS

....
....
....
....

CAPTAIN

Sailing Log Book ☸

DATE		DESTINATION	
WEATHER		FORECAST	
WIND		VISIBILITY	
SEA CONDITIONS		ETA	

TIME	COURSE	SPEED	DISTANCE	NAVIGATION NOTES	REMARKS

EVENTS / OBSERVATIONS

....
....
....
....
....
....
....

TIME COMPLETED		DAYS RUN	
AVERAGE SPEED		FUEL ON BOARD	

CREW & GUESTS

....
....
....
....

CAPTAIN

Sailing Log Book

DATE   DESTINATION

WEATHER   FORECAST

WIND   VISIBILITY

SEA CONDITIONS   ETA

TIME	COURSE	SPEED	DISTANCE	NAVIGATION NOTES	REMARKS

EVENTS / OBSERVATIONS

....
....
....
....
....
....
....

TIME COMPLETED   DAYS RUN

AVERAGE SPEED   FUEL ON BOARD

CREW & GUESTS

....
....
....
....

CAPTAIN

Sailing Log Book

DATE		DESTINATION	
WEATHER		FORECAST	
WIND		VISIBILITY	
SEA CONDITIONS		ETA	

TIME	COURSE	SPEED	DISTANCE	NAVIGATION NOTES	REMARKS

EVENTS / OBSERVATIONS

....
....
....
....
....
....
....

| TIME COMPLETED | | DAYS RUN | |
| AVERAGE SPEED | | FUEL ON BOARD | |

CREW & GUESTS

....
....
....
....

CAPTAIN

Sailing Log Book

DATE

WEATHER

WIND

SEA CONDITIONS

DESTINATION

FORECAST

VISIBILITY

ETA

TIME	COURSE	SPEED	DISTANCE	NAVIGATION NOTES	REMARKS

EVENTS / OBSERVATIONS

....
....
....
....
....
....
....

TIME COMPLETED

AVERAGE SPEED

DAYS RUN

FUEL ON BOARD

CREW & GUESTS

....
....
....
....

CAPTAIN

Sailing Log Book ☸

DATE _____   DESTINATION _____

WEATHER _____   FORECAST _____

WIND _____   VISIBILITY _____

SEA CONDITIONS _____   ETA _____

TIME	COURSE	SPEED	DISTANCE	NAVIGATION NOTES	REMARKS

EVENTS / OBSERVATIONS

....
....
....
....
....
....
....

TIME COMPLETED _____   DAYS RUN _____

AVERAGE SPEED _____   FUEL ON BOARD _____

CREW & GUESTS

....
....
....
....

CAPTAIN _____

Sailing Log Book

DATE

WEATHER

WIND

SEA CONDITIONS

DESTINATION

FORECAST

VISIBILITY

ETA

TIME	COURSE	SPEED	DISTANCE	NAVIGATION NOTES	REMARKS

EVENTS / OBSERVATIONS

....
....
....
....
....
....
....

TIME COMPLETED

AVERAGE SPEED

DAYS RUN

FUEL ON BOARD

CREW & GUESTS

....
....
....
....

CAPTAIN

Sailing Log Book ☸

DATE _____ DESTINATION _____

WEATHER _____ FORECAST _____

WIND _____ VISIBILITY _____

SEA CONDITIONS _____ ETA _____

TIME	COURSE	SPEED	DISTANCE	NAVIGATION NOTES	REMARKS

EVENTS / OBSERVATIONS

....
....
....
....
....
....
....

TIME COMPLETED _____ DAYS RUN _____

AVERAGE SPEED _____ FUEL ON BOARD _____

CREW & GUESTS

....
....
....
....

CAPTAIN _____

Sailing Log Book

DATE   DESTINATION

WEATHER   FORECAST

WIND   VISIBILITY

SEA CONDITIONS   ETA

TIME	COURSE	SPEED	DISTANCE	NAVIGATION NOTES	REMARKS

EVENTS / OBSERVATIONS

....
....
....
....
....
....
....

TIME COMPLETED   DAYS RUN

AVERAGE SPEED   FUEL ON BOARD

CREW & GUESTS

....
....
....
....

CAPTAIN

Sailing Log Book ⚓

DATE			DESTINATION		
WEATHER			FORECAST		
WIND			VISIBILITY		
SEA CONDITIONS			ETA		

TIME	COURSE	SPEED	DISTANCE	NAVIGATION NOTES	REMARKS

EVENTS / OBSERVATIONS

....
....
....
....
....
....
....

TIME COMPLETED		DAYS RUN	
AVERAGE SPEED		FUEL ON BOARD	

CREW & GUESTS

....
....
....
....

CAPTAIN

Sailing Log Book

DATE   DESTINATION

WEATHER   FORECAST

WIND   VISIBILITY

SEA CONDITIONS   ETA

TIME	COURSE	SPEED	DISTANCE	NAVIGATION NOTES	REMARKS

EVENTS / OBSERVATIONS

....
....
....
....
....
....
....

TIME COMPLETED   DAYS RUN

AVERAGE SPEED   FUEL ON BOARD

CREW & GUESTS

....
....
....
....

CAPTAIN

Sailing Log Book

DATE   **DESTINATION**

WEATHER   **FORECAST**

WIND   **VISIBILITY**

SEA CONDITIONS   **ETA**

TIME	COURSE	SPEED	DISTANCE	NAVIGATION NOTES	REMARKS

EVENTS / OBSERVATIONS

TIME COMPLETED   **DAYS RUN**

AVERAGE SPEED   **FUEL ON BOARD**

CREW & GUESTS

CAPTAIN

CPSIA information can be obtained
at www.ICGtesting.com
Printed in the USA
LVHW042242290920
667268LV00007B/101